Shadows, Skeletons
and a Southern Belle

Shadows, Skeletons
and a Southern Belle

Jilda Leigh

To order additional copies of this book, contact:
Xlibris Corporation
1–888–795–4274
www.Xlibris.com
Orders@Xlibris.com
120239

This book is dedicated to the following people:

For Rosebud (my Muse). Along the way, Buddy Boy and The Destroyer added life, color and characters to it. They also added life, color and characters to my life as well. Thank you my darlings.

For Baby Girl, for the reasons known only to her. Peace, outtie!

For Mom—I want to send my wholehearted thanks for her love and undying faith that I could (and would) accomplish anything I put my hand on.

For my Grandma for her constant support, love, and prayers.

Her mind was foggy. She wasn't exactly sure where she was. Then reality came crashing in. "What happened?" she thought to herself. "I'd planned everything out so carefully. I wrote a note. I took way too many pills. I even cut myself far deeper than I have ever cut myself before", she mumbled out loud. "What went wrong? Why am I still here?" Then, slowly, she began to sob. There were tubes coming out of her everywhere! IVs running to ensure she was hydrated. Hell, a nurse was checking on her every hour on the hour. This just couldn't be happening! But, it was.

There was an IV in each arm, and one in her left foot. She had a catheter. An oxygen tube was in her nose. Machines were humming and buzzing. The straps still hung loosely from the sides of the bed where she had been restrained. She continued to sob, looking around at the dismal surroundings. Her only thought—I failed again. "But, who had found me? Who had saved me?" she thought. "More importantly, why did they save me? WHY? Didn't they realize how much pain I was in? I mean, I just tried to kill myself, did they miss that clue?" she said to no one in the room.

Shadows crept in around her. They fit her like a glove. They were familiar, always bringing the sorrow and despair. She tried to turn on her side in the hospital bed, to no avail. She only cried harder and harder. The voices started to speak again, taunting her—laughing at her failure. The voices were always with her, like the shadows. They banged inside her head like a drum, always trying to get her attention.

She seriously considered ripping the IVs from her body, just to feel the pain, to know for certain this was real. But, something held her at bay. It wasn't the pain that caused her to pause; it was the idea of being restrained again. It was the fear, the fear of the unknown. The Skeleton named Fear that haunted her for decades. She thought back to her childhood, back to the beginning.

My name is Jilda Leigh. I am in the middle of my life, and am surrounding by shadows and skeletons. But, I'm getting ahead of myself a bit. I was born and bred in the South, by the grace of God. I was raised by a loving family, who like every great Southern family believes in God, grits, cornbread and sweet tea. I had a rather "average" childhood growing up in the South. I have a younger Bubba, who is my hero.

Of course, growing up—Bubba was my greatest adversary! I would threaten to murder him if he tried to kiss me, which he always did. We fought like all brothers and sisters do, but he's my Bubba. I can fight him, but nobody else better touch him! We had a good life living on the dirt road. Played roll-a-bat, hide 'n seek—all the normal childhood neighborhood games. Went to church on Sundays and Wednesdays. Fried chicken, cornbread, sweet tea. Don't get any better than that!

My mother, JD, grew up in the same area that I did. She played piano at an early age, and still does. She played in our church for a while, and we laugh now because lots of stuff she plays sounds like a hymn still. She has a knack for golf, killing house plants, tomatoes, and can cook anything! You never leave her table empty, unless you choose to. Everyone says their Mom's the best cook, but they're stretching the truth—my Mom truly is the best cook in the work. Ask anyone that's sat at her table.

My mom has worked hard all her life. She was a single parent trying desperately to make ends meet. She managed to put herself back through school while Bubba and I were still small and earned her Master's Degree. She would take classes during her lunch break, and study at night while we were asleep. She spent her entire career working for the state and worked her way up through the glass ceiling to being a power player before her retirement.

My grandparents played a large role in our lives. They still have the same 40-acre spread they had some 50 or 60 years ago. As long as I can remember, my PaPa raised Beefmaster cattle. That meant we had to haul in hay to feed them. Of course, he'd wait until the hottest day in August to do it. We laugh about it now, but it sure was tough then.

My grandma still lives in the same house. The family rallies around the matriarch. She's visited daily by children, grandchildren, great-grandchildren and great-great-grandchildren. Five living generations. And, grandma will tell you stories from long ago, if you can get her started! Her stories are the best. She'll wrestle you for the corner piece of cornbread, share her love of God with you, and talk to you about sports.

Oh! That's another thing. Sports. There's football, and everything in between football seasons. We'll watch just about every sport. All the women that is. Funny, but the men in the family don't seem to care too much for it. That's a head scratcher, ain't it?!

My aunt, GB, is my Mom's sister. She lives in the "low country". We import her up to the compound every week or so, so we can get our fix. She's very handy to have around, especially if you need to have something pressed. We've had some of the best times with her. And the funniest. Ask her about the wagon and the kerosene when you see her!

GB graduated from college, as did my mother. She holds a Master's Degree and taught special ed students in the public school system. Fits right in with this family! She does, however, have a great knack for listening and helping figure out what's going on inside my head sometimes.

So, that's my family and my childhood. At least, the parts of my childhood I remember the most. I don't have too many other memories until I get into late middle school or high school. That's when the deep sadness started. The shadows descended. I remember the skeleton Fear appearing then as well. Fear of people and things. Shadows hiding the unknown. The voices taunting and laughing at me when I failed or I felt insecure. The shadows and the skeletons fed my insecurities and shortcomings, even if they were only perceived.

I remember the Skeleton Fear with me the night I had to crawl out of the window to escape a drunken stepfather after he had beaten my mother and passed out. I remember Skeleton Fear being with me, following closely by the shadows of despair. Despair for my mother and us. Fear that he would continue, that he would find us somehow.

As with all abusive drunks, they are sorry later. This verbal abuse only added fuel to the voices, the skeletons, the shadows. My self-esteem took direct hits every time he took something out on me or Bubba—for some perceived or real offense. I grew to hate him. All my teachings from the Bible and church told me not to hate another human being. But I wasn't in control. The skeleton Fear was. I hated him. I hated what he was doing to my family. It wasn't his family, it was my family! He had to go. Or, I had to go. There was a showdown between me and the drunk.

All during high school, me and Bubba endured the drunk. We tried to stay out of the way, or in our rooms, or just gone. Skeleton Fear drove me to risky behaviors. I started doing drugs and drink beer. I thought it would hold the shadows and voices at bay. But, it only made me vulnerable and deepened the sorrow. At this point, I was still functioning (more or less) like a teenager—at least on the surface. I had no one I could talk to. Shadows hid my insecurities and Skeleton Fear kept my mouth closed.

It was during this time, after only of our nightly band practices, that I went on a binge of smoking and drinking. At one of the "usual" deserted spots, I ran into several other band mates. We continued to party, dance, and shoot off fireworks (a usual thing). It was getting late and one of the guys offered me a ride home. I didn't think anything of it because the shadows had fallen over his intentions. I'd ridden with him before, so it was no big deal.

We left the party and headed down my long dirt road, towards my house. He pulled over and tried to kiss me. I told him to knock it off and get me home before I got in trouble with the drunk. He just laughed, and tried to kiss me again. I said "no" again, which only made him madder. He grabbed my hair and pulled me from the car. He was standing behind me, the shadows falling around me. Skeleton Fear was laughing. The voices were laughing. He reached in front of me and started pulling my jeans off, tightening his grip in my hair.

He threw me to the ground, with him on my back. I was panicking. Skeleton Fear was roaring with laughter! I cried out, begging silently for the shadows to overtake me. When he was finished raping me, he kicked me in my back, got in his car and drove off. I laid there and sobbed for what seemed like forever. The voices were screaming for me to hurt myself.

I finally managed to pick myself up and start walking towards home. I knew the drunk would be waiting up to start his lectures and punishments. Fortunately, by the time I got home, he was passed out. I made it to my room, locked the door. The shadows finally descended. Pain wracked my body. I lowered myself into a scalding hot tub and sobbed. I sat there, holding my knees to my chest, until the water turned cold. Then, me, the shadows, Skeleton Fear and the voices went to bed. Skeleton Fear kept me from speaking of this event and this rape. The voices kept saying "no one will believe you—who would believe you?". Skeleton Fear kept me quiet, until now.

Then, I left. To an abusive husband. The only thing positive I got out of that marriage was my daughter, Baby Girl. She was beautiful, and the family adored her. I was so afraid of this small child. I didn't think I could care for her properly. I guess maybe Skeleton Fear told me I wouldn't be a good mom. Maybe my self-esteem took another hit. I don't know. So, I left her in the care of my Mom, and I left. Baby Girl being with my Mom was the best thing for her, at the time. At least I would do right by her; because I knew my Mom would move heaven and earth to be sure Baby Girl was cared for properly. I was a total mess, but I knew that Mom would ensure Baby Girl was cared for when I couldn't do it. I would continue to see her off and on, getting her for visits or having her stay with me. At some point (though I don't remember when), Baby Girl came to stay with me permanently.

For the next 20+ years, I allowed the shadows to consume me. The voices screamed at me to hurt myself. So, I did. Off and on, I drank too much, had sex with lots of people. I trashed my life and my body. I refused to see what was happening to me, because it hurt too much. I didn't want to feel anything. At one point I lived with the Paramedic. He was probably in as bad a shape as I was. Still, he was an ally. We partied too hard, drank too much. There was a constant flow of people in and out of the house.

I did things I hated myself for doing. Really hated myself for doing, but Skeleton Fear just egged me on, and the voices shouted "go go go"! I knew it was hurting my family, but I didn't want to have to face that. I couldn't face that. Besides, I had company—Skeleton Fear, shadows of doubt and sorrow, and voices. Oceans of sorrow.

Husband #2, the Constable, is a good man. He has a great heart. He just didn't want to be married to anybody. That was his only fault. He was a provider, adored his children, and mine. He just didn't want to be married. So, we parted company. We're still friends, and are still able to talk.

It's about this time that I was diagnosed with Diabetes. My aunt (who was a retired nurse) had been saying for years that I was a diabetic and my doctors were missing the diagnosis. She was right. I was so disillusioned. Not at having the disease, but that my whole life was now ruined! And, about a month after taking those stupid pills, I was placed on insulin shots to control my diabetes. I am a Type I Brittle Diabetic.

So now, here I am. I'm checking my sugar like 6 times a day and up to 11 or 12 shots a day—and it's still running rampant! I'm trying desperately to watch what I eat and drink to no avail. I was in a major depression cycle for sure! Little did I know it was actually Bipolar Depression. That was missed too.

I started to do research on diabetes, but not much. I was too disappointed. I didn't want to be informed. I wanted my life the way it used to be. But I was stuck with diabetes, literally. I had to watch what I ate, what I drank, checked my blood and take my insulin. And, I gained weight. The insulin I had to take packed on the pounds, that and the unhealthy eating and binge drinking. I hated the way I looked. I hated my body. I still dislike my body very much, but I have learned to live in my own skin. After all, this is the body that God gave me, whether I liked it or not. And, God doesn't make junk.

Skeleton Fear reminded me often that it might not be a good idea to try to change anything, but I had no idea what the outcome would be. I, of course, listened. So, I refused to exercise or stick to my diabetic diet. The diet and drinking and insulin continued to pack on the weight. God kept reminding me that my body was a gift and I needed to try harder, but I wasn't listening. Skeleton Fear and the voices and shadows kept pushing me the opposite direction.

Enter husband #3—the "Leaver". It's funny how this one still gets my goat. The Leaver was the great love of my heart. He destroyed me when he left. After almost 10 years of marriage, the Leaver decided he needed a different life. Turns out his different life turned out to be more difficult than he thought. Good for him! But, I digress. When the Leaver walked away, that's when the ocean tides rolled in. That's when the Skeleton Water appeared.

In October 2008, I got laid off my job. That's when Skeleton Insecurity became roommates with Skeleton Fear. Together, they made my life a living hell. Day after day, I submitted resumes to companies trying to find a job. Letter after letter of rejection poured into the mailbox. The voices howled with laughter. The Skeletons ganged up on me. I was tormented day and night. But, as a true Southern Belle—I pressed on. I packed it all away inside an emotional suitcase and tried to forget about it.

I continued to submit applications and resumes, and the rejection letters continued to pour into the mailbox. I became more and more depressed and despondent. I wished for a different life. I found no solace, and never slept unless I took my medication.

Skeleton Water and Skeleton Fear live together with Skeleton Insecurity. They are never separated. Skeleton Water fills me up, one drop at a time. I take stuff and hold it. A criticism, a hurt feeling, etc. Skeleton Water continues to fill me up until the tide feels like it's at the base of my throat. The voices cheer louder to add more water. The voices laugh and tell me to hurt myself. I try my best to keep them at bay.

In February, 2011—I first attempted to commit suicide. I took a ton of pills, cut my wrists, wrote some notes, and lay down on my bed. I finally gave in to the voices. They were ecstatic. Skeleton Water drained from my body—for a while. Skeleton Fear sat down in a chair—to watch me. Shadows crept back into the corners.

My daughter Baby Girl found me. I can't imagine, but I can guess that was the hardest thing she's ever had to witness. Well, that and watching the ambulance take me away.

I awoke in the ICU unit, with my Mom and GB looking at me. Stuck full of IVs and machines buzzing and humming. I remember now being shocked that I was still alive. I didn't want to be alive, I wanted to be dead and numb and not feel anything. I vaguely remember a doctor telling me something about me going to another hospital for additional treatment and me signing a paper. It was only a day or so later that I realized I had been committed to the psychiatric ward of one of our local hospitals.

Committed. The voices were howling with laughter. "You botched it, you moron", they said. Skeleton Fear got up from her chair. The shadows started crawling back towards me. Then, reality hit like a frying pan against the head. "I'm stuck here", I thought.

I was searched, organized, prodded, probed, checked, vampired, fed, and sent to lectures. Up at 6am, breakfast at 7:30am, lunch at 12:30pm, supper at 6:30pm, medicine at 9pm, and lights out at 10pm. "What in the hell is going on?" I thought. I was checked every hour, on the hour, during the night. Roll was taken at every meal, every class, and every activity. This is not going to be good. Skeleton Fear just smiled. The voices snickered.

I was given a handbook to read and complete. Handouts were given at lectures. Information was passed along so we would learn how to cope with our illness. "What illness?" I thought. The Skeletons and the voices only snickered.

After two weeks of this "participation", I was told I had improved and would be discharged. My diagnosis of Bipolar Depression was confirmed, along with OCD, and Generalized Anxiety Disorder. I was given scripts for medicines and an appointment with a psychiatrist. Then, I was patted on my head and sent on my way. I wasn't "cured". Nothing was different.

Shortly after my pardon from the warden, I start dating Ivan. We have supper most nights together, and he stays with me some. But, he doesn't put me first, so Skeleton Fear takes over. She tells me that he'll leave me, or Ivan has someone else.

Ivan and I argue a lot, but stay together. It's an on again, off again kind of relationship. At one point, it's off. I don't see him for about two weeks. We are both so miserable. Ivan admits there were other things that came first. I was shocked, and so was Skeleton Fear. The voices were angry. Ivan moved in, and things settled down. Or so it seemed.

Leap Frog! It's a year later. Skeleton Water and Skeleton Fear have a new roommate. Her name is Skeleton Cutter. You see, when I attempted suicide the first time, I cut myself. The voices rejoiced and danced, and I felt euphoric. So, Skeleton Cutter had a field day. When Skeleton Water filled me up, the voices would scream at me to hurt myself. Skeleton Cutter would do her worst. Scars crisscross my arms. Because cutting is addicting. Just like any other drug, or alcohol. But, each time I cut myself, the water would leave. The shadows would rush in and I would feel guilty and ashamed. I would hate myself for giving in, again.

Now, it's February 2012. I open my door to go out and check the mail. A man is standing there. Before I can mule kick the door, he's in the house. I've speed-dialed my Mom and told her someone was in the house. I can only assume she's heading my way because she always does when there is a problem.

My phone and glasses were taken from me and smashed. He used a box cutter to cut my forearms and ripped my shirt open to cut my chest. He busted my lip. He kept saying I was leaving with him, and I kept saying no. He cut me every time I refused. I guess my composure changed, because I told him "you're going to have to kill me right here where my momma can find my body".

He stabbed my chest and cut me very deeply. He then dragged me by my hair to the living room and dumped my purse on the floor. He took my keys, and then kicked me back into the kitchen. He stole my car. He left me in a heap in the kitchen, where my mother found me.

About 5 minutes after he left, the cavalry arrived in the form of my mother. Then, the police, fire trucks, ambulances, and helicopters were in the neighborhood. The neighbors were questioned but nobody saw anything. So much for our neighborhood watch program, huh?

The shadows engulfed me. They never left me after that. Skeleton Water continually filled me up. Skeleton Fear kept me in my house, locked in tight—constantly checking my doors and windows. Skeleton Cutter emptied the water—making me feel ashamed and loathing what I had become. As the next day dawns, it dawns on me the choices I made. The cuts on my arms are the visible reminders of the choices. Guilt sets in, along with a ton a self-doubt and a lack of confidence. What a viscous cycle.

The voices are with me now 24 hours a day, 7 days a week. They drive Skeleton Cutter to work her magic. The voices tell me how pathetic I am, how useless I am. They scream at me to continue to hear myself, only to laugh at me when I do.

I hold on for a few weeks, but I had to call the suicide hotline twice. I'm having terrible nightmares. I'm petrified and Skeleton Fear is delighted, clapping her hands with glee. Ivan doesn't know how to handle me because I zone out to another place. I don't know who he is if he tries to wake me up, or I try to fight him off.

Then I talk to my family and Ivan. I let them all know how much I'm struggling and if I don't go back into the psychiatric ward for a "tune up"—I will probably try to commit suicide again. I had been talking with my doctor for a while, and he had diagnosed me with PTSD. Now, I talk to my doctor and explained the situation, and away I go to "lock down".

So, it's back to the routine. I was searched, organized, prodded, probed, checked, vampired, fed, and sent to lectures. Up at 6am, breakfast at 7:30am, lunch at 12:30pm, supper at 6:30pm, medicine at 9pm, and lights out at 10pm.

Yes, the voices are still with me. They are mocking me for being so weak and "turning myself in". Skeleton Fear, Skeleton Insecurity, Skeleton Water and Skeleton Cutter sit down for tea—to wait for me to get out.

Only this time, it's different. Way different. I started to listen, really listen. I was still miserable. The shadows were starting to cover me, even in "lock down". The voices were still there, still taunting me. But I started to participate. I started to get pro-active about me and that made all the Skeletons angry.

I graduated from lock down, and came home. Only, it wasn't home. It was like someone else lived there. You see, in lock down you aren't given any therapy—you are only given a book and instructions on ways to cope. I didn't just need to cope, I needed therapy.

The Skeletons and the shadows moved back into their comfortable chairs, haunting me at will. The voices talked non-stop. Situations worsened my Bipolar Depression and OCD. PTSD nightmare (and day-mares) took their toll. I was struggling. Going down fast. I was trying to stay afloat against a tide that was determined to pull me under. I tried to explain to my family what was going on, but they couldn't understand.

Skeleton Cutter got her way a few times, releasing the waters. The voices cheered, and I felt wretched. Hadn't I learned anything? What good was I? What purpose was my life serving if all I did was suffer? I know, these are hard questions—but my mind races with these every day. What had I done wrong? Why was I being tormented and punished?

The PTSD nightmare continued, even though I was "supposedly" on medication for them. Why take it if it doesn't work? I'm still having them. Skeleton Fear stepped up and put her arm around me. "You might always have them" she said, walking away. The voices giggled.

Skeleton Cutter slashed out, bringing the blood to the surface. If the water wouldn't leave, at least the blood leaving the body would release something. Or so I thought. It only became more addicting. Each time I cut, I wanted more. Each time, the voice squealed for more cuts.

Back to where we began—in May 2012, I attempted suicide again. I'd planned everything out so carefully. I wrote a note. I took way too many pills. I even cut myself far deeper than I have ever cut myself before. I wanted to bleed. I wanted the pain. I welcomed it.

I wanted the shadows and the Skeletons with me. The voices were already with me. I wanted the whole dark party. But, again I was saved for a purpose. At the time, I didn't know the purpose, but I am finding it out as I go along.

I was told that Ivan and LG put me in a cold shower, but couldn't revive me. I was told the LG whispered "squeeze my hand if you are still with me" and I did it. I was told my Baby Girl was hysterical to find me like this again. That my family was distraught. My grandchildren were afraid I was gone.

That was the cold water being thrown on me. I was moved from ICU in one local hospital to the psychiatric ward I had been in twice before. Same routine as before. But this time, something was dramatically different with me. Skeleton Fear was standing outside. Why was she there? I still had Skeleton Water, Skeleton Insecurity and Skeleton Cutter and the voices, but why was Skeleton Fear not with me?

The shadows were slight, but they were still there. I believe they'll always be there. I still didn't receive any therapy there. In fact, I was "informed" it wasn't a treatment facility. I was there to learn how to cope with my illnesses. Whatever. I guess I'll have to do it on my own.

As any Southern Belle worth her salt in flip flops and pearls would do, I dug my heels in. I was determined to learn everything I could learn about my diseases, and myself. I would become a sponge—soaking up medical histories, psychological terms, anything I could get my manicured hands on. I wanted my life back. I wanted peace. And, I did learn—through listening and talking with other people, there are a great many resources available.

I started looking into my diabetes and how to manage it. I started reading everything was everything I could get my hands on. On the internet, in books, everywhere. Several powerful statements I found were in _Zen and the Art of Diabetes Maintenance._

"Of those persons with diabetes who have come to a deeper spiritual awareness, they definitely find that spiritual beliefs inspire them to manage their blood sugar better and, beyond that, to cultivate healthier lifestyles. They find their power from a more total understanding and deal with their lives in a much healthier manner."

"There are two circles in everyone's life. The inner circle is yourself and everything you can influence. The outer circle is those things you can't influence, even though they affect you. The more you ignore the inner circle and worry about the outer circle, the more life becomes a 'Donut of Despair'. But the more you focus on the inner circle and accept the outer one as beyond your control, the more power you exercise over your life."

You see, once you decide to educate yourself, you also have to educate the ones you love. They need to know what illnesses you have—what makes you tick. Your family and loved ones need to be just as pro-active as you are.

Your family and loved ones need to be educated, because they cannot cure you. They can listen to you, and love you. They can be supportive of you. Yes, they will agonize over it all, but you cannot help that. You have to realize that you have no control over how other people feel. You only have control over you. You must remember to tell them the positive things, as well as the negative things. That's when true progress and true communication are forged. That's when your family and loved ones begin to understand what you are going through.

There are six (6) things your family and loved ones need to know about you and your Skeletons and shadows—about your diseases and illnesses.

1) Acceptance: You need to know that your family and loved ones are not judging you for having a mental illness, for being sick.

2) Positive: You need positive reinforcement. I've already called myself every name in the book, so don't add yours to mine. Nagging or lecturing me will probably fall on deaf ears.

3) Respect: Even though I have a mental illness, I am still worthy of respect. I have to respect myself as much as I ask you to respect me.

4) Support: This is my illness/disease. Not yours. I don't need you to fix anything. You can't. I just need you to support me by listening, or sometimes not listening—just being with me.

5) Space: Sometimes, I just need the space in order to figure out what to do next. It doesn't mean I'm going to harm myself, or anything else. Maybe I just need the space and quiet to try to think and download.

6) Time: As with everything else, healing takes time. My disease will not change overnight. My medications don't work instantly. My moods flip flop from moment to moment, day to day. I have no control over that, and neither do you.

Having said all that, I know it's easier said than done. But, my family and loved ones will be a little better informed. Skeleton Insecurity is raging against the machine as I write this, because I have no idea if it will be accepted. But I'm going to try anyway.

Peace. That's what I'm looking for now. Peace and an organization to my life that allows me to have peace. But, peace is a hard thing to accomplish. I read recently a book called <u>Creating True Peace</u>. I found several things that were helpful.

> "Peace is the practice of mindfulness, the practice of being aware of our thoughts, our actions, and the consequences of our actions. Mindfulness is at once simple and profound. We have allowed violence to accumulate in us for too long because we have no strategy to deal with it. When we cannot handle our suffering, we spew forth our frustration and pain onto those around us. We are victims of our own suffering, but because we do not know how to handle it, we hurt others while we are in pain."

That means this Southern Belle has to accept responsibility for what I do. For whom I hurt. To try to find the tools I need in order to destroy the violence and rage within myself and move it out in a productive manner.

The monumental sorrow and sadness are the worst parts. They are still with me. I read recently in a wonderful book called _A Walk With Christ To The Cross_

"Worldly sorrow brings remorse, guilt and depression; godly sorrow is caused by the conviction of the Holy Spirit. Worldly sorrow leads to death; godly sorrow leads to a repentant heart."

I did feel remorse and guilt and depression. I did wish for death. But, I also felt the pull of the Holy Spirit throughout all these experiences. I chose not to listen, sometimes I chose to listen. At the time, I was mad at everything and everyone, including God. I felt forsaken. I felt lost.

Being a Christian—I didn't always follow the path God had set in front of me. Most of the time, I ignored it altogether. I needed to get back to my roots. I grew up in church. I accept Christ as my Savior at an early age. I needed to get my Southern Belle patoot back on the right path.

When I took that stand, Skeleton Insecurity walked outside to stand beside Skeleton Fear. I felt elated. I was making a stand. I was taking my life back! I don't know how. I don't know exactly where to start, but I'm doing it. I never wanted to return to that other life. I have read in the book _Made to Crave_ that if we forget to be self-controlled and alert, we are prime targets to fall back into that former life, and that's degradation. And, desperation breeds degradation. I didn't want that anymore.

Reaffirming my walk with God has helped me come to terms with several issues. Help me take stock of my life, so to speak. I need to get in better shape—if my body is a temple of God, I've wrecked it. Major housecleaning needs to be done. I have a 800-lb gorillas and elephants. These beasts have to go. I have to find the strength to move them, through prayer—and being still.

One area that continues to resurface is the relationship (or lack thereof) with my father. When Bubba and I were small, he left. I never knew at the time, but this would leave a hole that needed to be filled. He took more, so much more, with him that he would ever imagine (or me either). He severed all ties of communication. And, that's a heavy weight for anyone to bear, much less a child growing up.

I am not blaming all my problems on the absence of a parent, I am merely stating that his absence would continue resurface each Father's Day and his birthday. I continue to send cards and notes telling him I'd love to hear from him, but no response. It is at this point that I must say that he will have to answer for the non-response when he faces God on judgment day. I have continued to honor him.

I have already begun to take advantage of the information I have gained. I am doing extensive reading on my Bipolar Depression, PTSD and OCD diagnosis. There is a wealth of information on the internet and in the public libraries.

There are public organizations that have newsletters, meetings, etc. through NAME (National Alliance on Mental Health) at www.nami.org. If at all possible, join this organization. It is a tremendous help with tons of resources.

Meditation and Aroma therapy have been a great relief to me. It has allowed me to focus myself on "nothing" and download my brain. It gives me an opportunity to put Skeleton Water on a shelf. I just have to learn to leave her there.

Meditation (and Aroma therapy) help me find some sense of peace. Back to _Zen and the Art of Diabetes Management_, there are a couple of gems about meditation that are proving to be helpful.

- Meditation
- Solitude
- Exercise
- Awareness and Reading
- Prayer and Clarification

Those steps help me get centered, and clear my mind enough to find inner peace. There are a great list of benefits that are a road-map to self-improvement.

- Provides moral direction and clarity in our lives
- Gives us more confidence in our own inner strength
- Makes us feel more grounded and secure
- Makes us more conscious of life's meaning
- Improves our mental acuity
- Makes life seem more organized and sensible
- Serves as a kind of instinctive psychotherapy, but without the self-pity
- Gives us more intense humility
- Makes our perceptions more insightful
- Improves our mental and physical health as people with diabetes

I have checked out several websites, and checked out several books at my public library, on tai chi and yoga. One of the recreational therapy counselors suggested yoga as a good way to get exercise and "peace" for people who, like me, have a hard time getting around. Tai Chi seems to offer the exercise I need to meditate and de-stress. Maybe it will give me the flexibility to start walking again.

One part I found particularly helpful was through one of our group sessions. The counselor suggested we look at the 12 steps of AA. Instead of saying "alcohol" or "chemical"—say our particular illness. It has been extremely helpful to me. You can find the 12 steps through www.aa.org or your local library may have the 12 step book.

With constant vigilance, I have moved Skeleton Fear and Skeleton Insecurity from the table to the outdoors. Skeleton Water still rages from time to time. I still have to battle Skeleton Cutter every day. I have more research to do on that. The voices are still with me, as are the shadows. I am trying to ignore the voices, but they are screaming still. The nightmares are still here, and eerily real.

But, prayer and perseverance continue to hold them at bay for now. Matthew 5 sums up a great deal for me. I think of it was Jesus' pep talk to the disciples. It's also a great pep talk for me. I need some cheerleaders!

Bear in mind, this is one Southern Belle's account of how not to live your life. Several things I did learn: If you need to talk, talk. If you need help, seek help. There is no stigma attached to reaching out for professional help for depression, OCD, PTSD or any other illness. Always ask for forgiveness. Make amends where they are needed.

Today, I will trust that the events in my life are not random. I am going through exactly what I need to go through to learn something that will prepare me for the joy and the love that I am seeking. I am actively searching for positive things in my life that will move me to a better place in my life.

As I learned in church many years ago, God will ask you to carry only what you can carry. Many times I have thought I must be a giant. Not so, it was at those times that my God, my family and my loved ones carried my burdens for me. They carried me. They continued to love me and support me when I couldn't do it for myself. They refused to let me give up. They were my cheerleaders even when I couldn't hear them. Their prayers lifted me towards heaven when I needed it the most. For that, I am eternally grateful!

In the book *Zen for Christians*, I found some passages that made me take pause and truly look at the things that I was going through, and what I had been through. "Zen is a way of liberation from suffering—both the suffering we experience ourselves and the suffering we cause others." I had definitely been suffering, and continue to suffer. And, I had to admit that I had caused suffering to my family and loved ones. I had to find a way to deal with this.

In effect, Zen helps us let go of the things that get in the way of our path towards God's heart, and his will for our lives. That's the path I'm searching for, the path I want to take. Zen also teaches how to mediate and "sit still". As I already know from the Scripture, we are to "sit still and know that I am God". That's what we need to do. And if meditation helps me do that, I'm all for it.

Breathe. Listen carefully to everything. Pay attention to everything, including food you eat. The weather. Your posture. Your emotions. Be aware of your thoughts and pain. Are you daydreaming? What are you dreaming? Be mindful of everything and anything.

I have found that in order to create peace, through meditation, there are some steps I try to follow:

- I will practice truth, compassion, and non-judgment
- I will practice giving and receiving
- I will practice self-awareness
- I will practice prayer
- I will practice acceptance
- I will practice detachment from my negative thoughts
- I will practice right conduct.

Be well, my loved ones! You have my heart.

There are litanies of things you can do to lift yourself up. Here are just a few suggestions:

- Being a big brother or big sister
- Offering your services to the Red Cross
- Taking part in the activities run by churches, synagogues, fraternal organizations, and clubs
- Volunteering to work for a political candidate whose policies you believe in
- Work for your local Audubon sanctuary or state park
- Distributing Meals on Wheels
- Taking pledge calls for your public radio or television station
- Providing recreation activities for a local cerebral palsy support group
- Serving at your local Special Olympics

Through the book *Zen and the Art of Diabetes Management*, I found a great list of books that have proven to be helpful for me. Maybe they'll offer you some help, and hope.

- *The Art of Loving* by Erich Fromm
- *A Confederacy of Dunces* by John Kennedy Toole
- *Care of the Soul (A Guide for Cultivating Depth and Sacredness in Everyday Living)* by Thomas Moore

- The Art of Happiness (A Handbook for Living) by His Holiness the Dalai Lama and Howard C Cutler, M.D
- Ape and Essence by Aldous Huxley
- A Little Course in Dreams by Robert Rosnak
- Diabetes and Hypoglycemia: How You Can Benefit From Diet, Vitamins, Minerals, Herbs, Exercise and Other Natural Methods by Michael T. Murray, N.D.
- West with the Night by Beryl Markham
- The Heat Is On (the Climate Crisis, the Coverup, the Prescription) by Ross Gelbspan
- Leaves of Grass by Walt Wiltman
- The Best Spiritual Writing of 1998 edited by Philip Zaleski
- Desolation Angels by Jack Kerouac
- No Nature by Gary Snyder
- Awakening to the Sacred by Lama Surya Das
- The Poisonwood Bible by Barbara Kingsolver

Lessons in "Mindfulness"

I found several books on "Mindfulness" which is a way part of meditation and dealing with your illnesses. I hope some of these points will be helpful. They hit home with me.

- Meditation is a way of being, not a technique. Meditation is not about trying to get anywhere else. "It is about allowing yourself to be exactly where you are and as you are, and the world to be exactly as it is in this moment, as well.

- The astonishing thing is that nothing else needs to happen. We can give up trying to make something special occur. In letting go of wanting something special to occur, maybe we can realize that something very special is already occurring, and is always occurring—namely, your life unfolding in each moment in awareness.

- Each moment missed is a moment unlived. Each moment missed makes it more likely I will miss the next moment, and live through it cloaked in mindless habits of automaticity rather than living in, out of, and through awareness.

- Life is surpassingly interesting, revealing, and awe-provoking when we show up for it wholeheartedly and pay attention to the particulars.

- It is a radical act of love just to sit down and be quiet for a time by yourself.

- With our cell phones and PDAs, we are now able to be in touch with anyone and everyone at any time. In the process, we run the risk of never being in touch with ourselves.

- Maybe the fear is that we are less than we think we are, when the actuality of it is that we are much much more.

- Practice is not about doing, or "doing it right". It is about being—and being the knowing, including the knowing of not knowing.

- Healing is a coming to terms with things as they are, rather than struggling to force them to be as they once were, or as we would like them to be, to feel secure or to have what we sometimes think of as our own way.

- When a loss stirs great sadness and grief in us, after the wailing and the tears and the tearing of our hair, there comes a time when we have to fall silent. Silence is the ultimate prayer.

Dialectical Behavioral Therapy (DBT) was part of the classes I attended in "lock down". On my 3rd visit, I really paid close attention to the lessons. I took notes, I made journal entries of what I had heard and learned. There are several things I found extremely helpful—and gave me a sense of hope.

- Observe: Just notice the experience without getting caught up in the experience.
- Control your attention.
- Be alert to every thought, feeling and action.
- Notice everything that comes to your senses.
- Put words on your experiences.
- Put experiences into words.
- Participation: Become one with your experience, completely forgetting yourself.
- Do just what is needed in every situation.
- Practice your skills: Changing harmful situations; changing your harmful reactions to situations; accepting yourself and the situation as they are.
- See but don't evaluate. Be non-judgmental.
- Unglue your opinions.
- Accept each moment.
- Acknowledge, but don't judge it.
- Do one thing at a time.
- Let go of distractions.

- Concentrate your mind.
- Focus on what works.
- Play by the rules.
- Act as skillfully as you can.
- Keep your eye on your objectives.
- Let go of vengeance, useless anger.

Distract with "Wise Mind" Accepts:

1) Activities (hobbies, exercise, cleaning)
2) Contributing (volunteer work)
3) Comparisons (compare yourself to other with the same problems)
4) Emotions (read old letters, listen to emotional music)
5) Pushing Away (put the pain on the shelf)
6) Thoughts (paint, color, count to 10)
7) Sensations (squeeze a rubber ball, listen to loud music)

Self-Soothe the Five Senses

1) Vision (watch the stars, paint your nails)
2) Hearing (listen to beautiful music)
3) Smell (use lotions or a scented candle)
4) Taste (have a good meal, enjoy your favorite candy)
5) Touch (take a bubble bath, have a massage)

Improve the Moment

1) Imagery (imagine relaxing scenes; imagine hurtful feelings draining out of you like water out of a pipe)

2) Meaning (create a purpose, meaning, or value in the pain)

3) Prayer (Give prayers of thanksgiving)

4) Relaxation (Breathe deeply, take a hot bath)

5) One Thing at a Time (Focus everything on what you're doing at this one moment in time)

6) Vacation (Take a brief vacation; take a mental vacation; get in bed with chocolates and read)

7) Encouragement (Cheerlead yourself!)

12 Steps to Recover (taken from the AA Book of Recovery—paraphrased). Feel free to submit your form of "higher power" for God. My power is God:

1) We admit we are powerless over other people and compulsive patterns, and our lives have become unmanageable.

   Honesty in admitting the truth about ourselves and our situation is called surrender."

2) We come to believe that a Power greater than ourselves can restore us to sanity.

   "We are asked to open up our hearts and minds and to explore the options available to us in search of "a power greater than ourselves" that is willing and able to "restore us to sanity"."

   We don't lose our personal independence by seeking a "power greater than ourselves". Instead true independence can be seen as the personal freedom to make choices in life, combined with the necessary information and the spiritual health we need to make these choices wisely.

3) We make a decision to turn our will and our life over to the care of God as we understand God.

   Being spiritually grounded means having a sense of spiritual identity in a world where we have a place as a valued human being who has a right to be alive. We're not afraid that things might fall apart at any moment. We don't feel worthless or condemned. We feel we are a part of life. We feel inwardly secure—within our family, with friends, and in the community. We are able to trust our relationships to the care of God, even under stress.

Affirmations are a good way to build a concept of God which will give you hope, trust, and the power to live well, to enhance feelings of trust and confidence.

4) We make a searching and fearless moral inventory of ourselves.

An honest and balanced approach to facing ourselves as we really are today is what is wanted. It probably won't feel comfortable admitting some of what is true about ourselves, but we must be willing to be honest anyway. We have to see ourselves clearly in order to heal.

Few undertakings have greater potential. We are eliminating mental and emotional ruts that may have immobilized us for a long time.

a) Isolation/Intimacy: What is your ideal vision of being in touch with others? Is marriage or committed partnership an important value to you? How about your needs for privacy? Independence? Are you comfortable in one-on-one relating, or do you prefer group or family socializing?

b) Control/Structure: What are you limits and boundaries? What of yourself do you want to offer to others, and which others? Are you willing to ask for what you want?

c) <u>Obsession/Serenity</u>: What are you personal standards for moderation? What are the healthy sources of joy and pleasure that you celebrate in your life?

5) We admit to God, to ourselves, and to another human being the exact nature of our wrongs.

We are demonstrating our ability to act with real courage. Our faith ceases to be hypothetical. We are living it. For many, this is a very great change.

6) We become entirely willing to have God remove all these defects of character.

We can solve problems only by becoming willing to change something about ourselves. If recovery is to be a living experience and not just something we read and talk about, we're probably going to have to become willing to say goodbye to a lot of our old, habitual behaviors. A present character defect may be a former coping behavior that once was an important part of our survival kit, but in recover, it's excess baggage that needs to be thrown out.

7) We humbly ask God to remove our shortcomings.

Humility allows us to look at situations realistically. It allows us to be honest out how powerful or weak we and our resources are in relation to a task. Another method for cultivating humility while building self-respect is to school ourselves to remember where we came from before we found recovery and to count the blessings we have already received. When we rejoice in recovery, it's a form of praising and celebrating the presence of a living God in our lives.

8) We make a list of all persons we have harmed and become willing to make amends to them all.

We undertake the work that heals the relationships with other people. The promise of recovery is the promise of having these deep basic needs met, by the action of God as we understand God in our lives. Everyone in our circle of relationships is deserving of explanation and an attempt to make amends.

9) We make direct amends to such people wherever possible, except when to do so would injure them or others.

Making amends—to ourselves and to others—in recovery always means taking appropriate action. It takes courage. It also asks us to let God guide us when it comes to timing our amends.

a) All of our amends should reflect our own innermost values that we've identified.

b) When we make amends, we must stay within the healthy limits we have established for ourselves.

c) When we reach out to others, we need to remember to honor and respect their boundaries and values.

10) We continue to take personal inventory, and when we are wrong, we promptly admit it.

Stay self-aware in the present. No matter what we learn, it seems true that we keep only what we practice. As people in recovery, we have to learn to live life on life's terms. We learn to "take our own inventory" on an ongoing basis. We own our progress, as we admit and correct our failings and missteps. We accept responsibility for monitoring our own conduct. As we become increasingly aware of our own pitfalls, we find ways to walk around them. Self-inventory provides a "self-rescuing kit" to get us back on the path that leads in the direction we choose.

11) We seek through prayer and meditation to improve our conscious contact with God as we understand God, praying only for knowledge of God's will for us and power to carry that out.

This is a spiritual journey from a kind a spiritual death back into life. We who are the lost people rediscover our authentic, inner selves again. We move from the bleak, barren landscape of a failed existence back into a fruitful way of life, full of challenge and opportunity. How and when we pray is up to us, but we are assured of our right to a personal relationship with God through our understanding.

Seeking to discover and live out God's will for us is basic to our discovery. With prayer and meditation to keep in contact with God, we may truly come to walk in peace.

12) Having had a spiritual awakening as a result of these steps, we try to carry this message to others and to practice these principles in all of our affairs.

We offer to share the way of life we have found in the give and take of life's dance. What we give, we give voluntarily, offering to reach out our hand to the next person who reaches out for help. We also learn about humility. We come together in a health process that begins with admitting what we can't do for ourselves.

We share our experiences, including our pain, our unflattering insights into our own motivations, the feelings we fear others will not accept.

When we speak from our hearts, those who share a common problem hear us and are comforted. And in the act of personal sharing, we awaken more and more to our spiritual identity, validating and claiming ourselves.